# DIGGING FOR POOP FOSSILS

Kristina Lyn Heitkamp

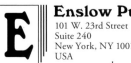
**Enslow Publishing**
101 W. 23rd Street
Suite 240
New York, NY 10011
USA

enslow.com

# Words to Know

**archaeologist** A scientist who studies prehistoric human history by examining body and trace fossils, as well as other artifacts.

**bezoar** A stomach stone of indigestible material.

**carnivore** An animal or human that eats meat.

**ecosystem** A community of species and plants that interact and live together in an environment, such as a rain forest.

**extinct** No longer living.

**fossil** The preserved remains of an animal or plant from the distant past.

**fossilized** Having turned into a fossil.

**herbivore** An animal or human that eats only plants or vegetables.

**paleontologist** A scientist who studies prehistoric fossils, such as dinosaur coprolites.

# Contents

# Everyone Poops

The average person poops roughly once a day and produces approximately 360 pounds (163 kilograms) of feces a year. Poop is mostly made up of water, about 75 percent. The rest is made up of bacteria, which makes turds stinky. Depending on your diet, poop can be different colors. Beets turn poop purple, while carrots or sweet potatoes give it an orange hue.

Everyone poops, even insects and fish. Animal poop, also called scat or droppings, comes in all shapes and sizes. Coyote

## FUN FACT

Whales poop 4 tons (3.6 metric tons) of iron-rich dung a day that fertilizes the ocean.

Poop is usually brown, but some food can turn poop colors. Spinach or kale makes poop green, and tomato juice can turn poop red.

Fossil hunter Mary Anning probably used a rock hammer to dig up fossils found in hard rocks.

scat is tubular and can be several inches long and full of animal hair. Caterpillars produce tiny square-shaped droppings found underneath trees. Cockroaches drop miniscule poop pellets that look like flecks of black pepper. Tropical parrot fish poop out tiny grains of coral that make up the white sandy beaches of the Caribbean and Hawaii.

With all waste produced by humans and animals, some poop turns to stone. Old piles of poo can harden into fossilized feces, also known as coprolites. The scientific name, coprolite, comes from the Greek words *kopros* (dung) and *lithos* (stone). During the early nineteenth century, a young fossil hunter and seller named Mary Anning discovered a coprolite along the southern shores of Great Britain. She thought the petrified poop was a bezoar—a stomach stone of indigestible material. But when she broke it open, the rock revealed fossilized fish scales and teeth.

# Left Behind

In the 1820s, English geologist William Buckland was digging around in a cave when he stumbled upon white grape-size blobs that looked like dog poop. He compared the rocklike stones with hyena poop at the zoo and discovered the blobs were the same shape and were made up of the same minerals. Buckland solved the mystery! He renamed the blobs coprolites and continued his journey into the study of ancient poop. He recognized that coprolites were little treasures of information. Buckland worked with other fossil collectors, such as Mary Anning. He discovered the fossils of a giant lizard, which later came to be known as the first discovered dinosaur.

## FUN FACT

One of the oldest human hairs was found inside a hyena coprolite.

William Buckland spent many years fossil hunting on horseback in England, Scotland, Ireland, and Wales. He coined the term "coprolite."

# Fossilized Feces

Coprolites form like any other fossil. Once the poop plops, it can either be destroyed, eaten, or decomposed. But if it survives, the stinky turd begins its journey to becoming a mineralized odorless stone.

When fresh feces falls into soft sediment, such as mud, and is buried, the layers of sediment stack up and can turn the feces into a coprolite over millions of years. If a poop drops in a cave, like the blobs Buckland found, it is safe from the elements, such as weather, and dries out. In special and rare

## FUN FACT

Sometimes, animal poo doesn't take long to fossilize, just a few hundred years.

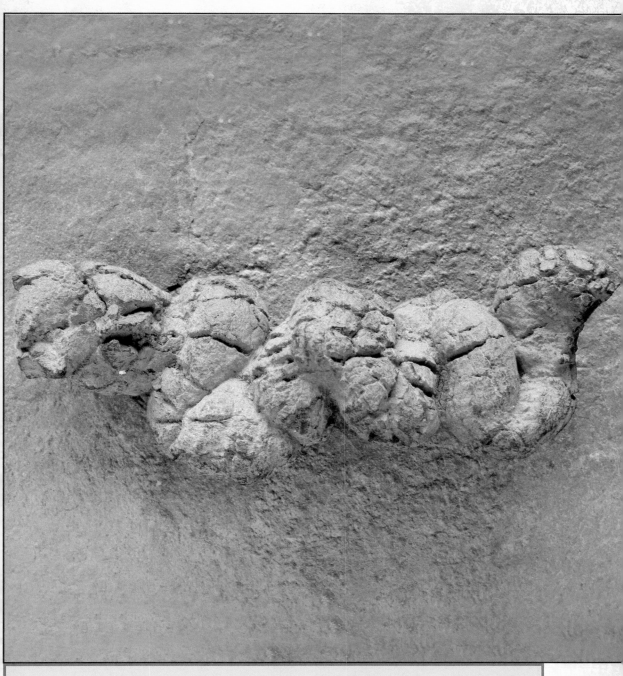

The shape of poop often matches the shape of the intestine. Corkscrew-shaped coprolites could come from ancient turtles or prehistoric sharks.

Found in southern Utah, this dinosaur coprolite is from the Mesozoic era. That's roughly 252 million years ago!

cases, poop will dry out inside a person's or animal's intestines.

One way to identify a coprolite is by its shape. Some fossilized poop looks like fresh poop, but looks can be deceiving. Ordinary rocks can also look like coprolites. Or sometimes the coprolite has been squashed into a shape that doesn't look like a fresh turd. Another clue to coprolite identification is what's inside. If the rock contains bones or plant material, then it could be fossilized feces. Coprolites come in all shapes, sizes, and even colors. Some people think that ancient poop is beautiful, including William Buckland. He had a tabletop made with coprolites that had been sliced and polished to display their unique beauty inside. Rumor is that Buckland would invite guests to dine at the table and later inform them what the table was made of. He was a bit of jokester.

# Dung Detectives

When examining a coprolite, researchers record the dung stone's shape, size, and texture. They will measure the stone and take photos. After evaluating the outside, scientists peek inside the poo. They slice off a tiny bit of the rock to place under glass to

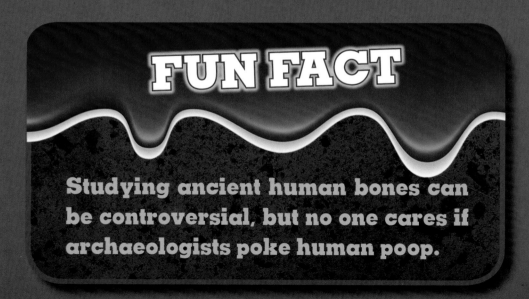

**FUN FACT**

Studying ancient human bones can be controversial, but no one cares if archaeologists poke human poop.

Paleontologist Karen Chin specializes in fossilized feces from dinosaurs. She studies coprolites for clues to ancient animals and ecosystems.

15

When scientists take a closer look at a dinosaur coprolite using a colored scanning electron micrograph, they can see colorful minerals inside.

closely examine the composition under a microscope. Researchers are very careful to not destroy the ancient evidence.

Coprolites reveal details that otherwise have been buried. The evidence found in fossilized feces helps build a better picture of how ancient animals and humans lived. Dung stones provide researchers with information about diet, behavior, and even disease. Coprolites can also provide clues to ancient ecosystems, including which animals lived together, what plants lived during the time and in that area, and even which animals ate other animals. By cracking open coprolites, scientists can find a time capsule of ancient life.

# Waste Is Not Wasted

It can be challenging to figure out what **extinct** creatures used to eat, but dinosaur dung tells scientists just that. Coprolites are windows into the prehistoric past. Two lumpy dino coprolites found in southern Utah revealed angiosperms, or flowering plants. This discovery told researchers not only that dinosaurs dined on the flowering plants but also that angiosperms existed at that time.

Inside a cave in southern Nevada, researchers found coprolites from an extinct giant sloth.

## FUN FACT

Toothless herbivore dinosaurs swallowed stones to help aid digestion, but some of those stones were coprolites.

A cross section of a dinosaur coprolite found in Utah offers evidence of what dinosaurs used to eat, including plants and other animals.

The cave was used as a home and a toilet. After analyzing the droppings, scientists discovered the bison-size giant sloth chomped on an orange flowered plant called desert globe mallow and a southwestern native shrub called Mormon tea.

# From Plants to Poop

Along with animal coprolites, early human poop also offers a glimpse into our prehistoric past. Club-swinging ancient humans, Neanderthals were thought to be meat-eating cavemen. In fact, some scientists had hypothesized that their strict meat-only diet is what lead to their extinction.

But examining their fossilized feces, researchers discovered large amounts of plant matter. The poop points to evidence that our ancient human cousins may have been omnivorous, eating

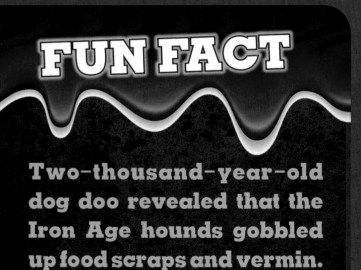

## FUN FACT

Two-thousand-year-old dog doo revealed that the Iron Age hounds gobbled up food scraps and vermin.

Early humans used primitive stone tools to scavenge for meat and to break up nuts and tubers to eat.

a diet of both meat and plants. They may have savored local grub in the area, such as berries, nuts, and tubers.

Ancient human coprolites not only uncover what our prehistoric relatives feasted on for dinner, but the dung stones also tell us stories about how they lived. Scientists investigated 1,600-year-old poop from two ancient indigenous peoples who lived on the islands of Puerto Rico. They discovered that one group favored maize, or corn—possibly answering a question of how maize first got to Puerto Rico.

The other group's poop contained no maize but had evidence of a fish diet. One ate fish while the other ate corn, despite the fact that they shared common resources. Specific diets are different all over the world today, based on customs, religion, and culture.

This ten-million-year-old coprolite is a little bigger than a large paper clip. This tiny fossilized turd is from a termite found in petrified wood.

# Disease and Death

Powerful nuggets of information, fossilized feces can show disease. More than 500 shark coprolites were found at a dried-up freshwater pond in southern Brazil. Scientists discovered tapeworm eggs inside the 270-million-year-old poop. Tapeworms are parasitic flatworms that can grow very long in the digestive tracts of fish, cows, dogs, humans, and other animals. Once the long snaky worm reaches adulthood, it unleashes eggs that are found in poop. A bundle of 93 tapeworm eggs were found in the spiral-shaped shark

## FUN FACT

The shape of fossilized feces can tell us about the shape of an animal's intestines.

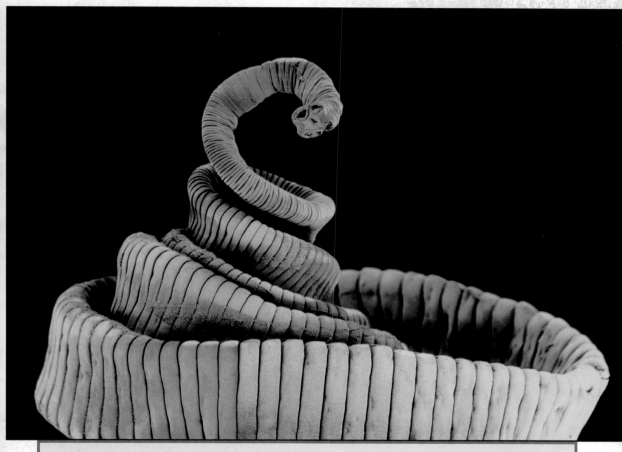

Tapeworms can grow over 100 feet (30 meters) long. Their heads have hooks and suckers that help them stay anchored in an animal's digestive system.

coprolite. Scientists couldn't say if the tapeworm infestation killed the shark. It is the earliest fossil record of the little buggers, millions of years before the first dinosaur pooped on Earth.

# Peek-a-Poo

Animals and people poop a lot, but finding coprolites is rare. If feces were easily fossilized, then scientists would find more poop than bones! A **carnivore's** dung droppings tend to fossilize faster than an **herbivore's** poop. This is because the meat eater's poop is higher in calcium, such as eggshells or bones. The richer mineral poo hardens quicker than its veggie or wood counterpart. Some carnivore coprolites can have whole intact bones buried inside or sticking out

## FUN FACT

In 2015, paleontologists discovered a rare find—fossilized poop inside a fossilized dinosaur.

A million-year-old coprolite shows a complete toe bone from a deer. Some fossilized feces are made up of undigested parts like bones, teeth, or scales.

Located in Alberta, Canada, Dinosaur Provincial Park is one of the most abundant dinosaur fossil quarries in the world.

the side, giving researchers clues that perhaps the carnivore wasn't an elegant eater and preferred to gobble down his prey without proper chewing.

Coprolites can be difficult to find because poop is often used in ways that destroys its composition. Some animals use poop to ward off predators. Other animals eat their own feces, scooping up the undigested bits of food to eat again. Sometimes poop just gets stepped on. Dinosaurs probably did not tiptoe around their piles of dung. But at the same time, it is surprising that scientists don't find mountains of fossilized dino doo. Where have all the piles of poo gone? Researchers discovered that dinosaur feces were likely devoured by an ancient cockroach, whereas today modern dung beetles and flies clean up poop piles.

# The Future of Feces

Different types of scientists, such as paleontologists and archaeologists, study coprolites and the clues they leave behind. To become a dung detective or fossil feces hunter, it takes curiosity, good detective skills, and an open mind to the information uncovered in coprolites. Get outside and explore. Keep a sharp eye out for evidence of the past. Follow tracks, pick up rocks and take notes on what you discover. Imagine the prehistoric past. Gems of evidence, coprolites help build a more complete story of our ancient history.

Don't be afraid to touch coprolites. You won't get your hands dirty, but you may develop an interest in the ancient past!

# Learn More

## Books

Coleman, Miriam. *Investigating Fossils* (Earth Science Detectives). New York, NY: Rosen Publishing, 2016.

Lunde, Darrin. *Whose Poop Is That?* Watertown, MA: Charlesbridge Publishing, 2017.

Masoff, Joy. *Oh, Ick!: 114 Science Experiments Guaranteed to Gross You Out!* New York, NY: Workman Publishing, 2016.

Owen, Ruth. *Paleontologists and Archaeologists* (Out of the Lab: Extreme Jobs in Science). New York, NY: Rosen Publishing, 2014.

## Websites

**Easy Science for Kids, "All About Fossils"**
*easyscienceforkids.com/all-about-fossils/*
Fun facts about fossils!

**Kids Discover, "Becoming Fossils"**
*www.kidsdiscover.com/teacherresources/becomingfossils/*
How fossils are made.

**Science News for Kids, "Dino-Sized Poop"**
*www.sciencenewsforstudents.org/article/dino-sized-poop*
How scientists estimate the size of dinosaur poop.

# Index

Published in 2018 by Enslow Publishing, LLC.
101 W. 23rd Street, Suite 240, New York, NY 10011

**Library of Congress Cataloging-in-Publication Data**

Names: Heitkamp, Kristina Lyn, author.
Title: Digging for poop fossils–Kristina Lyn Heitkamp.
Description: New York: Enslow, 2018. | Series: The power of
poop | Audience: Grades 3 to 5. | Includes bibliographical
references and index.
Identifiers: LCCN 2017020833 | ISBN 9780766090989
(library bound) | ISBN 9780766090972 (pbk.) | ISBN
9780766092778 (6 pack)
Subjects: LCSH: Coprolites—Juvenile literature. |Fossils—
Collection and preservation—Juvenile literature. | Feces—
Juvenile literature.
Classification: LCC QE899.2.C67 H45 2018 | CCD 560.75—
dc23
LC record available at https://lccn.loc.gov/2017020833

Printed in the United States of America

**To Our Readers:** We have done our best to make sure all
websites in this book were active and appropriate when we
went to press. However, the author and the publisher have
no control over and assume no liability for the material
available on those websites or on any websites they may link
to. Any comments or suggestions can be sent by email to
customerservice@enslow.com.